Science Tutor:
Earth & Space Science

By

GARY RAHAM

COPYRIGHT © 2006 Mark Twain Media, Inc.

ISBN 10-digit: 1-58037-332-1
13-digit: 978-1-58037-332-6

Printing No. CD-404046

Mark Twain Media, Inc., Publishers
Distributed by Carson-Dellosa Publishing LLC

Visit us at www.carsondellosa.com

Table of Contents

Introduction/How to Use This Book

Science Tutor: Earth & Space Science explores the nature of our amazing planet Earth and its place within the solar system and universe at large. *Part 1: Earth—A Wild and Changing Planet* looks at Earth's physical resources and internal structure, covering such topics as earthquakes, volcanoes, plate movements, the rock cycle, and fossils. *Part 2: Energy and the Atmosphere* reveals how solar energy churns through our atmosphere and provides the weather and climates so important to the biosphere. *Part 3: Sailing in the Hydrosphere* focuses on the critical importance of water in its several forms, how it cycles over time and space, and how human activities impact its quality. *Part 4: Earth's Cosmic Neighborhood* surveys other planets and objects in our immediate neighborhood, illustrates the causes of days and seasons, examines our moon's impact on tides and other phenomena, and looks at Earth's place in the larger universe. All of these topics parallel national science teaching standards for the Earth Sciences in middle school and above.

Key terms appear **boldfaced** in the text. *Absorb* sections introduce new concepts. *Apply* sections allow the reader to exercise his or her knowledge of the content and concepts by answering questions, filling in the blanks, and engaging in short activities. A few exercises will require additional paper. A calculator may also be useful, especially for *Sizes and Distances in the Solar System*. At the end of each section, the student is invited to "put it all together" and test his or her understanding of that section.

Because a lot of ground is covered in a short space, the visuals become especially important. Good illustrations and diagrams certainly do convey a large portion of the informational content and serve to organize ideas in a readily absorbable form. Some of the activities suggested in *Part 4* will require a light source, an apple, a pushpin, a soccer ball, and a tennis ball to help students visualize movements and relationships between Earth, the sun, and the moon. Add other visuals, like a map of the solar system and galaxy. If available, and if time permits, lead students to relevant websites, such as the following: United States Geological Service at www.usgs.gov/ and www.usgs.gov/education and National Aeronautics and Space Administration at www.nasa.gov/.

1

Part 1: Earth—A Wild and Changing Planet
A Planet in Constant, if Slow, Motion

Earth rocks! It also slips, folds, tilts, and breaks in a process called **deformation**. Over periods of years, centuries, and millennia, these Earth movements can result in earthquakes, volcanic eruptions, and other processes human beings sometimes witness directly. Over long periods of time, entire mountain ranges can rise, valleys can form, and rivers can sculpt rock into strange and delightful forms.

All of this motion results from **stress** induced from heat deep within Earth's core acting on the relatively cool and brittle layer of rocks forming Earth's crust. Continental crust averages 32 kilometers (km) in thickness, although it can be 70 km thick beneath mountains. Oceanic crust tends to be about 8 km thick. Stress can result in forces of **compression**, **tension**, or **shearing**.

When rocks are compressed, put under tension by being pulled apart, or sheared from side to side, the rocks may **fracture**, **fault**, or **fold**. Fractures are simple cracks like the kind that form when mud dries, but on a much larger scale. Faults are places where rocks break and then slide against one another—usually either up and down or side to side. When compression causes one side of a faulted rock to slide over the other, a **thrust fault** results, which may change the normal layered pattern of rocks.

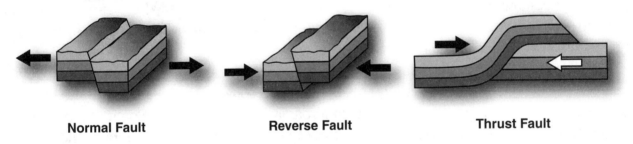

Normal Fault   **Reverse Fault**   **Thrust Fault**

Sometimes, as in an area of western North America called the Cordilleran mountain region, entire **fault-block mountain ranges** may rise. Down-dropped blocks may create **rift valleys**, like Death Valley in California.

When rocks are hot enough or under enough pressure, they may fold instead of break. An **anticline** folds upward, while a **syncline** dips downward. The Appalachian Mountains of eastern North America display many anticlines and synclines.

Hot liquefied rock called **magma** beneath the crust may cause rock to form a **dome**, rather like a rocky zit. Many of the rounded peaks found in the Black Hills of South Dakota are dome mountains of this sort.

Plateaus are large areas of flat land raised above the general level of surrounding land. Plateaus may result from domes whose tops have been gnawed flat by the forces of erosion or from large blocks of land thrust up between faults, as is the case for an area in the Rocky Mountains called the Colorado Plateau, which includes parts of Colorado, New Mexico, Utah, and Arizona.

Satellites provide pictures that clearly show that Earth resembles a very wrinkled hide upon which we humans crawl, like ants on an elephant's back. Let's look more closely at some of the surprises our "elephant" provides as it twitches and squirms beneath us.

Shakin' With Quakes

The shaking, trembling, or rolling movements usually caused by bodies of rock slipping past each other at faults are called **earthquakes**. About one million earthquakes occur annually, but most go unnoticed. A few hundred of these make significant changes on the earth's surface, and a dozen or so cause severe damage and loss of human life.

Continental faults like the San Andreas in California may cause widespread damage by bringing buildings and bridges down, destroying highways, and breaking gas lines, which then catch on fire. Quakes at sea caused by the vertical motion of rocks can displace tons of water and create waves called **tsunamis** that create havoc when they reach land. The ocean-bottom quake west of Indonesia on December 26, 2004, created the tsunami that killed at least 145,000 coastal residents and tourists. The point beneath the earth where the rocks move is called the **focus** of a quake. The **epicenter** is the spot directly above the focus on the earth's surface.

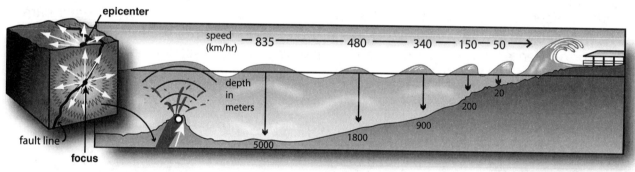

Rock slippage creates several kinds of **seismic waves**. **Primary**, or **P waves**, move quickly, pushing and pulling their way through solid rock, liquids, and gases. P waves speed up through dense rocks and slow down in less dense material. **Secondary**, or **S waves**, move more slowly and only through solids. The slowest waves, called **L waves**, occur at the earth's surface and cause the most damage because the earth moves up and down as they pass.

Seismographs record earthquake waves with a pen suspended on a weighted wire that hangs above a rotating drum of paper. When the earth moves, the drum moves, and the pen traces a spike. The height of the tallest spikes are used to calculate the strength of a quake on the **Richter scale**. Quakes usually fall within a range of 1 to 10 on this scale, with one being a very mild quake, and anything over six being very destructive. The Richter scale is logarithmic, so each number represents a quake about ten times stronger then the one below it.

Scientists constantly work at finding ways to accurately predict when and where earthquakes will occur.

Some predictors that have proved useful are:
1. changes in the speed of P and S waves;
2. slight changes in the tilt of Earth's surface;
3. slight rising or sinking of land near a fault;
4. movement of water up or down in wells; and
5. unusual behavior by animals.

Volcanic Cauldrons

The historian Will Durant used to say "Civilization exists by geologic consent, subject to change without notice." This observation was inspired, in part, by volcanic eruptions that not only kill people close to them, but may affect climate on a worldwide scale for many years, as did the eruption of Tambora in 1815 that made 1816 the "year without a summer," especially in northern Europe and North America.

Volcanoes are exit holes at Earth's surface for molten rock called **magma** that finds its way to the surface by melting rocks above it or oozing through cracks. Once exposed at the surface, magma becomes **lava**. Hot, fast-moving dark lava with lots of iron and magnesium called **pahoehoe** (pah-HOH-ay-hoh-ay) solidifies into wavy, rope-like patterns. **Aa** (pronounced "Ah-ah," because of what you say when walking over it) is cool, slow-moving lava that forms spiky chunks. Both of these kinds of lava are produced during fairly slow and mild eruptions of dome-like **shield volcanoes** like Mauna Loa in Hawaii.

Violently erupting volcanoes often produce a light-colored lava high in silicon and aluminum compounds that becomes rhyolite, or granite. **Cinder cone volcanoes** have narrow bases and steep sides. Lava containing lots of water and carbon dioxide creates a light and "holey" rock called either **pumice** or **scoria**, depending on its exact composition. **Composite volcanoes** like Mount Vesuvius and Mount Etna in Italy produce alternating layers of rock and lava.

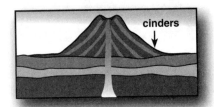

Cinder Cone Volcano

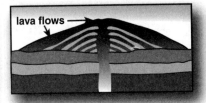

Shield Volcano

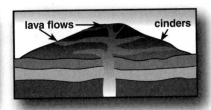

Composite Volcano

Volcanoes may produce **dust** the texture of flour, **ash particles** about the size of rice grains, or shoot out **volcanic bombs** the size of boulders. Golf-ball-sized projectiles are called **cinders**. Volcanoes belch these goodies from deep within the earth through holes called **craters**. Lakes sometimes form in the basins of craters of inactive volcanoes. A broad crater three times wider than it is deep is referred to as a **caldera**.

One of the most impressive calderas is the entire area of Yellowstone National Park in Wyoming. This ancient volcano is currently **dormant**, but it shows evidence of several past eruptions. It's currently past due for an eruption. **Extinct volcanoes** show no activity and are often weathered down to their old magma chambers. **Active volcanoes** are those that have erupted sometime during recorded history. Mount Saint Helens in the state of Washington erupted suddenly in 1980 after many years of dormancy.

Slowly erupting volcanic areas in Earth's past have produced vast areas of layered lava extending over thousands of square miles. These areas are called **volcanic traps**.

Patterns of Earth Activity and Plate Tectonics

Volcanoes and earthquakes may occur unexpectedly, but not without a pattern. Many volcanoes erupt in an area that encircles the Pacific Ocean, often called "**The Ring of Fire.**" Similarly, a string of mountains in the mid-Atlantic Ocean that stretches north and south for 80,000 km exhibits much geologic activity.

Looking at a map of the world, people have often been impressed by how many of the continents look as if they would fit together like the pieces of a jigsaw puzzle. The "fit" of South America and Africa is particularly striking. Because continents seem like such fixed features on the earth, this observation seemed at first like a curious coincidence, but later geological discoveries showed that something more significant was going on: for example, the rocks and fossils on the east side of South America and the west side of Africa are precisely the same age and fit together exactly as if they were once-joined coal fields, and an ancient mountain range lines up perfectly. The same kinds of ancient fossils turn up not only in South America and Africa, but in Australia, India, and Antarctica. The implication is that these continents were once joined in a supercontinent, which scientists have named **Pangaea**, but it was unclear how such continental movement could happen.

The clues to the mechanism of continental drift came together in the 1950s and 1960s as geologists began studying the Mid-Atlantic Ridge, mentioned above. Researchers discovered that magma from deep within the earth welled up along this ridge, adding huge volumes of new crust to our planet by causing the sea floor to spread. They were able to show that ocean crust was youngest near the ridge and grew steadily older as they sampled away from the ridge in either direction. This sea floor spreading was accompanied by subduction or burial of ocean crust at deep trenches that lay either within ocean basins or near some continental margins. Both areas turned out to be "hot spots" of geological activity.

The driving force of all this activity consists of currents created within Earth's rock mantle by the intense heat of Earth's core. The mantle flows like hot taffy carrying the lighter crustal rocks above it on a slow-motion ride of millimeters or centimeters per year. The crust has fractured into seven major **tectonic plates** (and a number of minor ones) that sometimes collide and grind past each other. **Divergent** plate boundaries move apart; **convergent** plate boundaries crash together, often forming mountains like the Himalayas; and **strike-slip** boundaries, like that between the Pacific and North American Plate along the California coastline, struggle past each other, causing many earthquakes in the process.

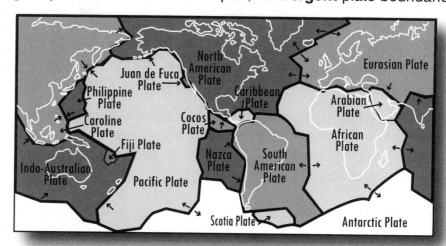

Minerals and Their Uses

Our earth cooks **minerals** in her volcanic cauldrons. Minerals come together to make the rock foundation of all her amazing and beautiful wrinkles. So, what's a mineral? A **mineral** is any naturally occurring, non-living, solid with a specific chemical composition and crystal structure. Although the industrious geologist can identify 2,500 different kinds of minerals, he or she will only see about 100 frequently. Less than 20 are widely distributed. This is partly because 98.5% of Earth consists of just eight elements: oxygen (46.6%), silicon (27.7%), aluminum (8.1%), iron (5%), calcium (3.6%), sodium (2.8%), potassium (2.6%), and magnesium (2.1%). The most common rock-forming minerals are quartz (SiO_2), calcite ($CaCO_3$), augite (Ca, Na), hematite (Fe_2O_3), micas, and feldspars.

Minerals can be identified by several physical properties:

1. Many minerals possess specific **colors** like the green of malachite and the blue of azurite. Other colors vary with heat, cold, pollution, radiation, and the presence of impurities in otherwise clear minerals like calcite.
2. **Luster** is the way in which a mineral reflects light. **Metals** shine with a metallic luster. **Nonmetals** may appear silky, pearly, dull, or even brilliant, but never shiny.
3. A mineral's **hardness** is measured by its "scratchability" on a scale from 1 to 10 called the **Mohs scale**. Talc, given a number of 1, is very soft, while a diamond scores a perfect 10. In the field, a geologist uses some common items to test hardness: a fingernail has a hardness of 2–2.5; a knife blade is 3–4; glass is 5–6; and a steel file or nail is 6.5–7.
4. Minerals produce a smudge, or **streak**, of a characteristic color when rubbed on an unglazed porcelain tile (like a bathroom tile).
5. Minerals each possess a characteristic **density** or mass per unit volume.
6. Minerals possess 1 of 6 basic **crystal shapes**.

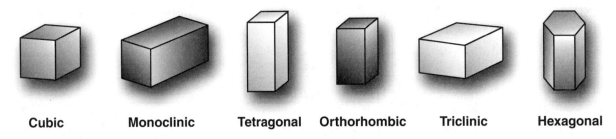

| Cubic | Monoclinic | Tetragonal | Orthorhombic | Triclinic | Hexagonal |

7. Minerals break in specific ways. Micas **cleave** into thin sheets. Quartz **fractures** with shell-like shaped edges. Salt, or halite, breaks into **cubes**.
8. Certain minerals may have **special properties** like the magnetism of magnetite or the radioactivity of uraninite.

Mineral ores provide us with all the raw materials to make virtually everything from toothpaste to CD players and hair dyes to motorcycles. In addition, especially striking crystal mineral forms like rubies, sapphires, diamonds, and other **gemstones** appeal to our sense of beauty.

Igneous, Sedimentary, and Metamorphic Rocks

The minerals formed deep within the earth combine in various ways to form the hard solids we call **rocks**. Volcanic glass and opal also form rocks, although they don't have a crystalline structure. Geologists classify rocks based on how they form. Igneous rocks form from hot magma. Sedimentary rocks form from particles that settle out of water or collect through the action of wind, like sand dunes. The weight of accumulated particles, along with mineral-laden water cements everything together. Metamorphic rocks are rocks of any type that have been transformed by heat and pressure.

Igneous rocks: Geologists classify igneous rocks based on the kinds of minerals in them, along with their shape, size, arrangement, and distribution. Light-colored igneous rocks tend to possess more clear quartz, while dark-colored igneous rocks contain more augite, which displays gray-green colors. **Extrusive rocks** cool and harden on Earth's surface. Examples include the noncrystalline volcanic glass called obsidian, as well as basalt, which has fine-grained interlocking crystals. **Intrusive rocks** cool more slowly beneath the earth, producing coarse-grained rocks with easily seen crystals like pegmatites and granites. Porphyritic rocks look a bit like chocolate-chunk ice cream with big crystals scattered in a field of small crystalline minerals.

Igneous: basalt

Sedimentary rocks: Take fragments of pre-existing rocks, mash them together, and you get **clastic rocks** like **conglomerates**, **breccia**, **shale**, and **sandstone**. Conglomerates are often called pudding stones because river-smoothed pebbles get cemented together like a very hard raisin pudding. Shales are called mudstones because they form from fine-grained muds. **Organic rocks** were once living organisms. Many **limestones** form from deposits of shells, and compressed plant remains become beds of **coal**. **Chemical rocks** result from minerals left behind after water evaporates. These include rock salt (**halite**), **gypsum**, and **some limestones**, like the beautiful deposits formed in caves.

Sedimentary: sandstone

Metamorphic rocks: Take a rock, any rock, heat it up between 100° and 800°C or so, squeeze it, and you get something new. Shale or volcanic tuff becomes **slate**. Granite turns into **gneiss** (pronounced "nice"). Chalk (fine-grained limestone) becomes marble. Metamorphic rocks are often layered or **foliated**, like **schists**, slates, and gneisses. These rocks tend to break along these layers, or bands. **Unfoliated** (unbanded) metamorphic rocks include **marble** and **quartzite**.

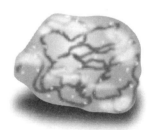

Metamorphic: marble

Name: _____ Date: _____

The Rock Cycle

As you may have guessed from the discussion of rock types, rocks slowly transform from one kind to another as they are beaten by the forces of wind and water, buried, pushed, and shoved back beneath the crust, and heated, re-cooked, and belched from an active volcano. The hardest granite mountains wear away to become washed into lakes and oceans at about the same rate as your fingernails grow. Ocean sedimentary rocks last only a certain period of time before plate tectonics subducts them below the crust to be refashioned. This process is called the **rock cycle**, even though it is a cycle that follows no particular order.

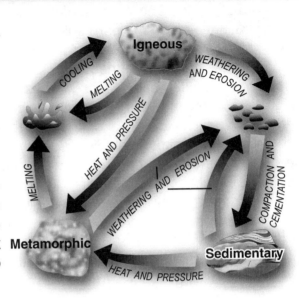

Directions: Look at the diagram above and review page 7 to to fill in the blanks.

1. Igneous rocks become sedimentary rocks by:
    A. _Weathering_ and _erosion_.
    B. _compaction_ and _cementation_.

2. Sedimentary rocks can become metamorphic rocks by applying _heat_ and _pressure_, or they can be converted directly to igneous rocks if they _melt_ to become magma.

3. To become an igneous rock, magma must _Melt_ and _cool_.

4. When an artist carves a marble statue, he is working with a kind of _metamorphic_ rock.

5. T or (F?) Limestones are only formed from the remains of once-living creatures.

6. Rocks are composed of one or more _minerals_.

7. Put some heat and pressure on granite and you'll get _gneiss_. (Isn't that nice?)

8. A conglomerate is a kind of _gneiss_ sedimentary rock, while coal is an example of a(n) _clastic, organic_ sedimentary rock.

Fossils: Images From Life's Past

Now and then, a living thing manages to die in such a way that its remains are at least partially preserved in sedimentary rocks as **fossils**. Animals may also leave **trace fossils** behind in the form of tracks, tunnels, and excrement (poop). Someday, soda cans and action figures could become trace fossils.

Should you ever wish to improve your chances of becoming a fossil, here's a plan:

1. **Hard things** like bone, teeth, and tree trunks often fossilize well. As a vertebrate with a calcium-phosphate skeleton and enamel-coated teeth, you come equipped with excellent hard parts.

2. **Get buried quickly** under muck or a massive cave-in so that scavengers don't gnaw your bones to shreds, and wind and water don't destroy them. Creatures living in areas of sedimentary deposition like a river or ocean basin have a better shot at fossilization than mountain-living animals or plants—unless the latter are buried by a volcanic lava flow.

3. You have to get lucky, too, (if that's the right word!) and **be preserved someplace where your rocky remains don't get "rock recycled" too quickly**!

Fossils may form in a variety of ways:

1. Some creatures fall or get stuck in **tar**—a natural asphalt like that found in California's LaBrea Tar Pits. Insects often get stuck in tree sap that later hardens to **amber**. Sometimes animals may be **freeze-dried** in a glacier or on a mountaintop, like the 5,000-year-old "ice man" found in the Italian Alps.

2. When creatures get buried in sediments or by lava and later soak in mineral-laden water, they may literally turn to stone and become **petrified**. This kind of preservation may show detail down to the level of individual cells, like Arizona's petrified forest.

3. Animals or plants buried in lake sediments or swamps that slowly decay while being squeezed and slow-cooked will become **carbonized**. They look a bit like rock road kill.

4. Sometimes only a creature's shape is preserved as either a **cast** or a **mold**. Eruptions of Mt. Vesuvius in Italy have covered humans with lava. The lava hardens into a mold, while the body inside decays. If the mold later fills with sediment or more lava, a cast forms that reproduces the original body shape.

5. Trace fossils like footprints or tunnels dug in moist sand will sometimes dry quickly, be buried, and then compressed into stone. Fossil dung may get covered quickly and later petrify.

However they are formed, fossils provide clues to the 99% of Earth's organisms that have become **extinct** (no longer exist). **Paleontologists** study fossils to reconstruct Earth's living past.

Weathering, Erosion, and Deposition

On some planets, the rock cycle proceeds very slowly, if at all. On our atmosphere-coated world, however, various agents break down rocks in a process called **weathering**. Many of these same agents move soil and other rock by-products around and **deposit** them elsewhere in a process called **erosion**.

During **mechanical weathering**, rocks are physically broken down by the results of **changing temperatures**, the **action of living things**, **gravity**, and the **abrasive forces** of wind and water. Alternate heating and cooling of rock surfaces cause uneven expansion of rock, resulting in pieces of rock breaking off near the surface. This **exfoliation** slices off slabs and flakes parallel to the rock surface. Water seeps into cracks in rocks. Because water expands when it freezes (unlike most substances), alternate melting and freezing slowly expand cracks until the rock breaks. Plant roots grow into the cracks of rocks (and beneath sidewalks), eventually prying them apart. Gravity causes landslides. Water tumbles rocks in streams until they are smooth, and wind sandblasts mountains to rubble and piles up sand into dunes. Rivers move rock debris and soil to the sea, and glaciers plow soils and rock in a slow-motion farming operation.

Chemical weathering changes the chemical composition of rocks. Water, often called the universal solvent, can dissolve many substances. Atmospheric carbon dioxide dissolves in water to form **carbonic acid**—a natural version of soda pop. Carbonic acid turns feldspars into clay and slowly dissolves limestones. Earth's atmosphere also contains 20% **oxygen**, a powerful source of chemical change. Oxygen greedily combines with iron to form **iron oxide** (rust). Coal combustion pours lots of sulfur dioxide into the air, which turns to sulfuric acid in water. **Acid rain** quickly chews on rocks, metals, and monuments, like the ancient temples of Greece. Mosses and lichens make acids that dissolve rock.

How fast weathering occurs depends on several factors. Certain **stable rocks** resist weathering, but stability often depends on climate. Both limestones and granites are quite stable in dry climates, but they break down fairly rapidly in tropical climates. Limestones succumb to the carbonic and sulfuric acids that form in water. Granites have a high feldspar content, and as mentioned above, feldspars turn to clays when attacked by water. Buried rocks get less exposure to air, so will survive intact longer. The less surface area a rock has exposed to the agents of weathering, the longer it will take to break apart.

Eventually, though, gravity, wind, running water, glaciers, and the action of waves have their way, beating down mountains and washing the by-products into the sea. Fortunately, our old Earth has enough fire in its belly to make new mountains and continue the process for a very long time.

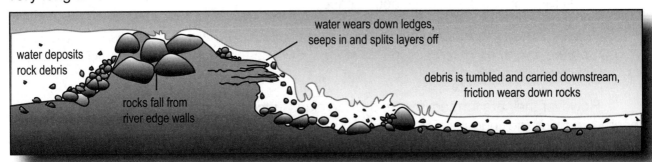

water deposits rock debris

water wears down ledges, seeps in and splits layers off

debris is tumbled and carried downstream, friction wears down rocks

rocks fall from river edge walls

Name: _____ Date: _____

Part 1: Earth—A Wild and Changing Planet
Putting It All Together

CONTENT REVIEW

1. When rocks are put under great stress, they may _____,
_____, or _____.

2. T or F? The seismic waves called secondary, or S waves, are the most destructive during an earthquake.

3. In order of increasing size (smallest to largest), the kinds of materials ejected from volcanoes are: (circle one)

   A. Bombs, cinders, ash, dust
   B. Cinders, bombs, dust, ash
   C. Dust, ash, cinders, bombs
   D. Ash, dust, cinders, bombs

4. T or F? California's west coast is on a strike-slip plate boundary.

5. Name four physical properties used to identify minerals.

   A. _____   B. _____
   C. _____   D. _____

6. Briefly explain the difference between igneous, sedimentary, and metamorphic rocks.

   _____
   _____
   _____

7. T or F? A fossil is always the petrified remains of a living thing.

8. If a rock containing iron rusts, this is an example of _____ weathering.

9. _____ rocks resist weathering.

10. _____ rocks cool and harden on Earth's surface.

Name: _____ Date: _____

Part 1: Earth—A Wild and Changing Planet
Putting It All Together (cont.)

CONCEPT REVIEW

1. Would you expect the rock cycle to occur more slowly or more quickly on Mars than on

   Earth? _____ Explain. _____

   _____

2. Would an animal today be more likely to become fossilized in Colorado or Louisiana?

   _____ Explain. _____

   _____

3. If you found a conglomerate rock, you could safely say: (circle one)

   A. The action of moving water was involved in its formation.

   B. It was formed in a volcano.

   C. It was reheated and transformed from sedimentary rock.

   D. It was an intrusive rock.

4. If you wanted to find out the hardness of a rock in your backyard, name three com-

   mon items you could use to estimate hardness. _____,

   _____, and _____

5. If you visited an area that had a lot of earthquake activity near a range of high mountains, what

   kind of plate boundary might you expect to be near? _____

6. If you were visiting a beach and heard reports of an earthquake 100 miles offshore, what

   should you do and why? _____

   _____

7. T or F? Mountains are always formed by faulting.

8. T or F? Weathering may be occurring somewhat faster today than a thousand years ago

   because of the burning of coal.

Part 2: Energy and the Atmosphere
Earth's Heat Engine

Earth, because it can hold a layer of gases, or **atmosphere**, close around itself, experiences **weather**. Weather is the day-to-day behavior of the atmosphere. The vast quantity of heat energy that radiates from the sun provides the driving force for weather.

The **radiant energy** that bursts from the sun's surface can do several things when it hits Earth's atmosphere:

1. It may bounce off dust particles and molecules of water vapor and end up back in space or scatter within the atmosphere.

2. Its heat energy may be absorbed by clouds of water vapor. A portion of the sun's radiant energy is **ultraviolet (UV) radiation**. A large share of UV light is absorbed by the **ozone layer**—a layer of oxygen gas made up of three atoms of oxygen (O_3) instead of the normal two. This absorption is important for living things today, because UV radiation is highly energetic and can cause mutations and cancers in living tissue.

3. Radiant energy may reach Earth's surface and be absorbed. That energy can then enter the atmosphere through **conduction**, **convection**, or **radiation**.

A small amount of heat energy moves directly from Earth's surface to the mass of air immediately in contact with it—a process called **conduction**. The majority of heat energy, however, transfers to air in a process called **convection**. The energy causes air molecules to speed up and spread out, making that air less dense. Such warmed air rises. Cooler, denser air sinks

until it, too, is warmed. These **convection currents** carry heat energy in churning cells of moving air. Lastly, some heat energy passes into the atmosphere directly as **infrared radiation (IR)**. This is the same kind of radiation that warms you from a heat lamp or keeps a burger warm on the waitress's counter before she serves it.

Infrared radiation, unlike the original radiant energy from the sun, can't pass through the atmosphere, but instead gets absorbed by water vapor, carbon dioxide, methane, and other gases. They serve as a heat blanket, keeping heat in, just like the panes of glass in a greenhouse. This impact of gases, like carbon dioxide, in trapping heat within Earth's atmosphere is called the **greenhouse effect**.

Heat transfers easiest when the sun is directly overhead and the angle of solar radiation is 90° to Earth's surface. Thus, areas of Earth at the equator get hotter faster. At shallow angles (higher **latitudes**), the heat energy of solar radiation spreads over a greater area.

Temperatures are measured with a **thermometer**—a device with a narrow column of liquid that expands and rises when heated and contracts and falls when cooled. The freezing and boiling points of water are 0° and 100°, respectively, on the **Celsius** temperature scale and 32° and 212°, respectively, on the **Fahrenheit** temperature scale.

Changes in Air Pressure

If the Earth were an apple, its atmosphere would be as thick as the apple's skin. In reality, the Earth attracts a layer of air 800 km thick. The weight of all of that air results in pressure on anything beneath it. The precise air pressure at any given point on the planet depends on the density of air there, which is the mass of air within a certain volume (**Density = Mass/Volume**).

Density, in turn, is affected by three factors:

1. **Temperature:** As temperature rises, air molecules spread out so there is less mass in a given volume. Air pressure decreases. Cooler air can hold more gas molecules and thus, it is denser, producing higher air pressure.
2. **Water vapor:** Moist air is less dense than dry air because the weight of water molecules (H_2O) is less than the weight of the other major atmospheric gases, nitrogen (N_2), and oxygen (O_2). Moist air masses will have a lower air pressure than corresponding dry air masses.
3. **Elevation:** The farther one moves from the surface of Earth, the less air there is above them, so air pressure declines with increased elevation. In grams per cubic centimeter (g/cm^3), air pressure at sea level is 1,034.

Barometers measure air pressure. The early mercury barometer was nothing more than a narrow, inverted tube suspended in a pan of the metal mercury. As air pushed down on the mercury in the pan, it forced it up the narrow tube. The higher the mercury in the tube, the higher the air pressure.

Modern **aneroid barometers** have a metal chamber with nearly all of the air removed. When air pressure changes, the chamber expands or contracts, moving a pen on a lever arm that records movement on paper or moving a dial on a scale.

Air masses moving toward each other often create areas of **high pressure**. This pressure prevents warm, moist air from rising to form clouds. Thus, high-pressure areas often mean fair weather. Air masses moving away from each other create **low-pressure** zones where warm, moist air can rise and form rain clouds.

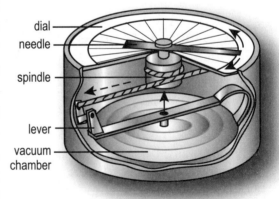

Aneroid barometer

Blowin' in the Wind

Cool, dense air swoops under warm and rising air of lower density to create **wind**, or air on the move. Air always moves from high to low areas of pressure. Some winds, however, blow persistently and over great distances because we live on a huge spinning globe that heats unevenly.

Local winds: Some local winds reflect the fact that land heats faster than water, but water retains its heat longer. Go to the beach during the day, and you will often feel a cool breeze coming off the water. This is because the land heats quickly, warming the air above it, which rises. Cooler, moist air from over the water slides beneath the rising air, creating a **sea breeze** on an ocean beach. At night, the water stays warm after the land has cooled, resulting in an **offshore breeze**. The name of a breeze always tells the direction from which the wind is blowing. A southwest breeze blows from the southwest toward the northeast. Some "local" winds can be quite regional (and seasonal) in nature, like the warm and wet **monsoon winds** that bring heavy rain to Southeast Asia when they blow from ocean to land.

Global winds: Solar energy pours more efficiently into the atmosphere at the equator where it enters from directly overhead. In general, warm tropical air tends to flow toward the cool poles, while polar air slides toward the equator. But the earth is large and spins, complicating things. Earth's spin results in a **Coriolis effect**, where winds are shifted in opposite directions in the Northern and Southern Hemispheres. Earth's air masses break up into cells that result in certain consistent wind patterns.

Doldrums: Consist of mostly very calm air in a band over the equator.

Trade winds: Occur between latitudes 30° north and south. These warm winds blow back toward the equator in usually clear skies.

Prevailing westerlies: Occur between 40° and 60° north and south latitudes, consisting of cool air, usually moving quickly toward the poles from west to east in both hemispheres.

Polar easterlies: The westerlies rise and cool between 50° and 60° latitude and collide with cold polar air. The wind is deflected west by the Coriolis effect, creating cold, fairly weak winds blowing from east to west.

Polar Easterlies — 90°N
60°N
Prevailing Westerlies — 30°N
Trade Winds
Equator 0° — Doldrums
Trade Winds
30°S
Prevailing Westerlies — 60°S
Polar Easterlies — 90°S

Jet streams: Were not discovered until the 1940s. These are narrow bands of air that zip along at an altitude of 12 kilometers. They move about 180 km/h in the summer and 220–350 km/h in winter, dipping here and there in seasonal and/or daily patterns. The swirling **eddy currents** they cause in lower air masses may result in storms.

Cloud Nine and Other Vaporous Collections

Heat up liquid water, and it will change phases, turning into water vapor. **Humidity** is a measure of the amount of water vapor in a given mass of air. Our planet's atmosphere can hold as much as 14 million tons of water at any given time. Not bad, Mother Earth!

Relative humidity is the amount of water an air mass is holding relative to the maximum amount it *could* hold when completely **saturated**. Air saturated with water vapor has a relative humidity of 100%. Meteorologists read relative humidity with a **psychrometer**—a pair of thermometers, one wrapped in a wet cloth and one wrapped in a dry one. When the air is saturated, the thermometers will read the same, but the **wet bulb** thermometer will read at a lower temperature as its moisture evaporates in unsaturated air, losing heat energy. Charts based on the difference between wet and dry bulb readings reveal the relative humidity.

Warm air holds more moisture than cool air. As warm air rises and cools, it reaches a point where it will be saturated with water. At this point, the **dew point**, water will condense on any handy particle in the air. A crowd of such water droplets makes a cloud. Clouds are described by their shapes. Puffy and fluffy cumulus clouds, often with flat bottoms, form at an altitude of 2.4 to 13.5 km. Smooth and gray layered stratus clouds form at 2.5 km and often bring light rain and drizzle. Stratus clouds at ground level are called **fog**. Feathery **cirrus** clouds form at 6–12 km and consist of ice crystals.

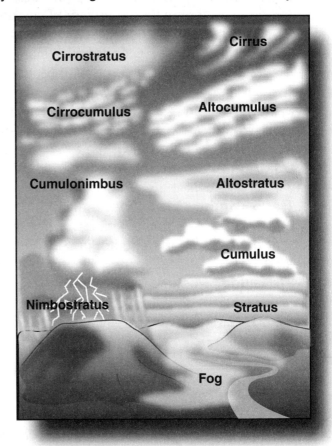

Of course, clouds sometimes form in perverse mixtures that look like combinations of the basic three types. The picture at right shows some of the "hybrid" clouds.

When cloud droplets get about a million times heavier, they are forced to obey the pull of gravity, and they fall as **precipitation**. Rain, of course, is liquid water, usually measured in a calibrated container called a **rain gauge** with straight sides and a flat bottom. When the air is cold enough, water vapor immediately turns to solid snow, made up of beautiful six-sided crystals. **Sleet** is partially frozen water that reaches the ground in winter, but may melt before hitting the ground in summer. When ice pellets form and get tossed around in a high cloud until several successive layers of water freeze, they may get heavy enough to fall as **hail.** Hail pellets vary from the size of rice grains to small melons or softballs. Ouch!

Making Sense of Weather Patterns

When the sun pumps lots of heat into Earth's atmosphere, it creates **air masses** with many different **temperatures** and **humidities**. As these air masses bump and jostle each other, they create **weather**. **Meteorologists** define air masses by *where they form*. **Maritime air masses** assemble over oceans. **Continental air masses** build over land.

North America contends with four types of air masses:

1. **Maritime tropical** air masses form over the ocean near the equator and can bring hot, humid summers or stormy winters if they bang into cold, northerly air heading south.
2. Cool and moist **maritime polar** air masses form over the Pacific Ocean and the North Atlantic.
3. A summer air mass called the **continental tropical** forms over Mexico and brings hot air to the southwestern states.
4. The **continental polar** air mass forms over northern Canada and may cause the mercury in thermometers in northern states to nosedive.

Points of contact between air masses are called **fronts**. A **warm front** forms when warm air meets and rises above a cold air mass. As the warm air rises, its temperature falls, making it less able to hold water, which results in rain. When a cold air mass overtakes a warm air mass and shoves its way underneath, the warm air rises quickly. These **cold fronts** often result in more violent storms. When cold and warm air masses meet but don't move much, a **stationary front** results, which may produce extended rains. Two cold air masses may collide and push a warm air mass up between them. The weather in such **occluded fronts** is hard to predict.

Rainstorms and **snowstorms** result from the collision of different fronts. **Nimbostratus** clouds form when a warm front moves in and rises over cold air, often resulting in heavy rain or snow. A **blizzard** results when wind speeds exceed 56 km/h and the temperature is less than -7°C.

Thunderstorms form when a cold front moves in and meets a warm front. High, **cumulonimbus** clouds produce thunder, lightning, and sudden air movements called **wind shears**, which are dangerous for planes.

Spinning air masses called **cyclones** form when cool air swoops in to replace rising warm air in a region of low pressure. **Anticyclones** form in high-pressure areas with cold, dry air that spirals out in a direction opposite to cyclones, usually bringing clear, dry, and fair weather.

Cyclones called **hurricanes** form powerful storms over tropical oceans. Similar storms that form over the western Pacific Ocean are called **typhoons**. The centers, or **eyes**, of such storms are calm, while around them air hurtles by at 480 km/h.

Whirling funnel clouds over land called **tornadoes** form in low cumulonimbus clouds. **Waterspouts** form over water. Both types of storms may cause great damage with winds that spin up to 95 km/h.

Name: _____ Date: _____

Predicting the Weather

Once upon a time, people had to rely on Grandpa's arthritis pain to know when the weather was going to change, but now **meteorologists** (weather scientists) can rely on **local weather observers**, **weather balloons**, **satellites**, and **weather stations** all over the world to do a better job. Meteorologists create **weather maps** to show the weather in a particular region or area that provide information on **wind speed and direction**, **cloud cover**, **precipitation**, the **position and direction of fronts**, and **air pressure**.

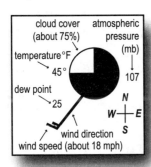

Clever little symbols provide all this information in condensed form on official weather maps. For example, the information provided by a weather station will look like the box at left.

Notice that the circle in the center is blackened to show the percentage of cloud cover. To the upper left is temperature. The upper right shows **barometric pressure** in **millibars** (mb) or **inches of mercury** (1 mb = 0.03″ of mercury). A line sticking out from the circle shows the direction *from which* the wind is blowing. Wind speed is given by a series of lines coming off the wind direction indicator. Each full line represents 9–14 mph wind speeds.

Now look at a complete weather map in the figure below. Note the symbols on the wavy lines indicating **cold fronts**, **warm fronts**, **stationary fronts**, and **occluded fronts**. The semicircles on warm fronts and triangles on cold fronts always point in the direction of the movement of the front.

Isotherm lines (*iso* means "equal" and *therm* refers to temperature) show areas across the map region where the temperature is the same. **Isobars** show lines of equal barometric pressure.

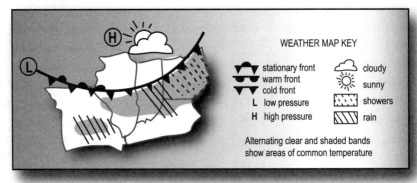

APPLY:

Explain why the symbols for stationary fronts and occluded fronts look like they do. (Refer to page 17.) _____

_____

_____

_____

_____

Persistent Weather: Climate

 When people talk about the typical temperatures and precipitation for a particular area over a long period of time, they are talking about the area's **climate**. Both temperature and precipitation are affected by several factors that lead to a rich variety of climates on our "water world" planet.

Temperature varies largely because of three things:

1. **Latitude** is the distance north or south of the equator measured in degrees. As you've learned, Earth gets warmed up the most where the sun is directly overhead and sunlight hits the ground at a 90° angle. This occurs on the equator at 0° latitude. Average temperatures get progressively colder as you move toward either pole.

2. The **elevation**, or altitude, of an area is its distance above sea level. The air thins out (becomes less dense) as you climb a mountain or rise in a balloon. Thinner air holds less heat, so temperature decreases with a gain in altitude.

3. The **temperature of ocean currents** directly affects the temperature of the air above them. In general, warm ocean currents flow away from the equator, and cool currents flow toward the equator. Major currents like the **Gulf Stream** (see map at right) can significantly warm the air near landmasses that would otherwise be quite cold.

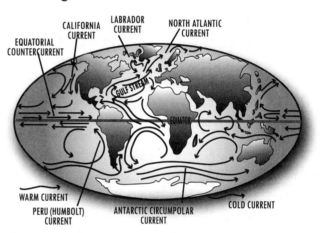

Precipitation varies because of two major factors:

1. **Prevailing winds** are winds that blow more often from one direction than any other. They may be warm or cold and carry varying amounts of water, depending on whether they are blowing off water or land (see page 15). Sometimes deserts can even exist near large bodies of water if the prevailing winds are off a large landmass; such is the case with the Sahara Desert in northern Africa.

2. **Mountain ranges** serve to block, or at least alter, the flow of prevailing winds. Air must rise to get over a mountain, and rising air cools and becomes incapable of holding as much water. Therefore, the side of a mountain facing the prevailing wind (the **windward side**) tends to get a lot of moisture. The **leeward side** of the same mountain gets sinking air stripped of most of its moisture, often resulting in a desert in the mountain's so-called "**rain shadow**." Such is the case for the Sierra Nevadas of western North America and the desert-dry Great Basin east of it.

Climate by the Zone

The earth can be divided into three large **climate zones** based on average annual temperatures and defined by latitude.

Some of the factors discussed on the previous page led to many regional variations on each zonal "theme."

1. **Polar**, or **arctic**, **climate zones** exist between latitudes 90° and 60°. Here, near either pole, there is no summer, and the average yearly temperature remains below 0°C. If you travel to the icecaps of Greenland or the continent of Antarctica, you will experience a polar zone.

2. **Temperate zones** extend from latitudes 60° to 30°. Inhabitants of these climate zones experience seasonal swings in temperature. Annual average temperatures can vary from 5°C to 20°C. Expect to find inland deserts that can be quite hot and dry during the day, but cool, or even cold, at night.

3. The **tropical zone** bands the earth from the equator at 0° to 30° on either side of the equator. Expect high temperatures, high humidity, and no winters. Even during the coldest months, temperatures never drop below 18°C. Because the trade winds (see page 15) blow east to west, you will find deserts on the west sides of north-south trending mountain ranges. The Atacama Desert of Chile and Peru is exceedingly dry, for example, and cold because of cool offshore ocean currents.

Within each zone, **marine** and **continental climates** provide variation. The large bodies of water of marine climates give up moisture to winds, providing more precipitation. Temperatures don't vary as much because water is stingy when releasing heat. Summers tend to be warm (rather than hot) and winters mild. Dryer continental climates exist within large landmasses. Temperatures swing more wildly from high to low. Summers may be hot and winters quite cold.

While we owe our climate zones to Earth's round shape, the annual variation in temperature and precipitation we call the four seasons—spring, summer, fall, and winter—results from the fact that our planet is tilted at an angle of 23.5° relative to the sun. When the Northern Hemisphere of the Earth is tilted toward the sun, that hemisphere gets more heat and experiences summer, while the Southern Hemisphere deals with winter. Six months later, the situation is reversed. In the months between summer and winter, both hemispheres get the same amount of sunlight and experience either spring or fall, depending on whether the transition is toward summer or winter. **Spring** in the Northern Hemisphere occurs March 20 or 21, and **autumn** begins September 22 or 23 (see page 39).

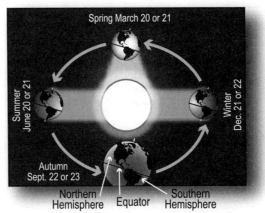

Season dates are for the Northern Hemisphere.

Part 2: Energy and the Atmosphere
Putting It All Together

CONTENT REVIEW

1. Solar energy can enter the atmosphere and reach Earth's surface through

   _____, _____, and

   _____.

2. Earth's atmospheric pressure depends on the density of air, which, in turn, de-

   pends on _____, _____, and

   _____.

3. T or F? A sea breeze is wind blowing from land to water.

4. When air has become completely saturated with water, it has reached its

   _____ _____.

5. T or F? Severe weather is most often associated with cold fronts.

6. The weather station symbol used on weather maps contains all of the following informa-

   tion *except*: (circle one)

   A. Barometric pressure.
   B. The position of storm fronts.
   C. The percentage of cloud cover.
   D. Temperature and wind speed.

7. The temperature in a particular area will vary depending on its _____,

   height above _____ _____, and how near it might be

   to _____.

8. T or F? The temperature is always hotter in a tropical climate zone than in a temperate

   climate zone.

9. T or F? When the Northern Hemisphere is experiencing winter, the Southern Hemisphere

   is experiencing spring.

10. The side of a mountain facing the prevailing wind is the _____ side.

Name: _____   Date: _____

Part 2: Energy and the Atmosphere
Putting It All Together (cont.)

CONCEPT REVIEW

1. T or F? During an "ice age," the earth is completely covered by snow and ice.

2. Although Mars has a much thinner atmosphere than Earth, you would still expect air temperature to (increase, decrease) as you climb higher on a mountain. (circle one)

3. Why would anything that decreases the ozone layer be a problem for living things?

    _____

    _____

4. Explain why captains of sailing ships often had trouble sailing close to the equator.

    _____

    _____

5. Explain how a psychrometer measures relative humidity.

    _____

    _____

6. What type of clothes should you pack on a winter trip to Florida if you hear that a maritime tropical air mass is moving in? _____

    _____

7. Look at the following weather station symbol: ⟍ From what direction is the wind blowing?

8. What would happen to the climate of New England if the Gulf Stream no longer passed by its shores? _____

    _____

9. Miguel and Juanita both live in a polar climate. Miguel lives near a seashore, and Juanita lives far inland. Who will most likely experience colder temperatures? _____

    Why? _____

    _____

10. T or F? The most direct sunlight falls on the equator.

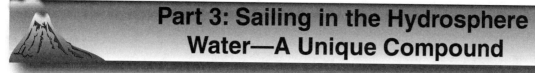

Part 3: Sailing in the Hydrosphere
Water—A Unique Compound

 Water. We drink it, swim in it, sail on it, bathe in it, and flush it. Our bodies are essentially giant bags of water propped up with the minerals in our bones. We tend to forget just how special a compound water is. Scientists refer to the two-thirds of Earth's surface covered by oceans as the **hydrosphere**.

Water is a **covalent compound** made up of one molecule of oxygen *sharing a pair of electrons* with two atoms of hydrogen. (Recall that **ionic compounds**, like table salt (NaCl), usually form crystals, and one atom *gives up its outermost electrons* to the other.) The giant oxygen atom in water, however, like a big brother or sister, tends to hog more than its share of electrons. Thus, the oxygen end of a water molecule carries a slight negative charge (from the extra electrons), and the hydrogen molecules carry slight positive charges from their partially exposed nuclei. As a result, water is said to be a **polarized molecule** with a big negative end and two small positive pips stuck on at an angle of 105°.

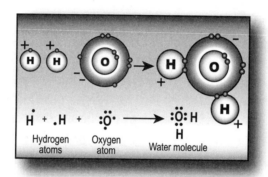

"So what?" I heard you ask. Because water molecules are polarized, the negative oxygen end of one molecule tends to form weak, **hydrogen bonds** with the two positive hydrogen atoms of another molecule. This makes water molecules "sticky," so they tend to clump together. Because of this, it takes more energy for water molecules to be broken apart and **evaporate** to gaseous water vapor. Water is one of the relatively few compounds that remains liquid at "room temperature." Chemical reactions—ones that we depend on every day—occur more easily when chemicals are **dissolved** in water. The polar properties of water also help make it an excellent **solvent**. The charged ends of water molecules are very good at tugging apart the charged atoms in ionic compounds, for example. Water dissolves so many substances that it is often called the **universal solvent**.

The polarity of water molecules also allows them to pull apart the atoms of various acids into charged **ions**. These hydrated (water-coated) ions increase their ability to interact in the chemical reactions of living things.

Water also combines with various compounds to form **hydrates**. When the salt $CaCl_2$ is spread on dirt roads, it first combines with water vapor in the air to form a hydrate, then it absorbs enough additional water to dissolve and moisten the dirt so it doesn't blow around as dust.

As we will soon see, these are only a sampling of water's many unique properties.

Water's Changing Phases

Water is so common, important, and unique that it has been made the standard reference for many things. The unit of heat energy called the **calorie**, for example, is the amount of energy needed to raise the temperature of 1 millimeter of water (1 gram) 1°C. Few other substances require this much energy to change their temperature. Water is said to have a **high specific heat**. It requires more energy to break water's hydrogen bonds and get those molecules moving.

It also takes a lot of energy to melt one gram of ice or freeze one gram of water. Water has a **high latent heat of fusion**. Water has the highest **latent heat of evaporation**, meaning that it requires 536 calories for every gram of water evaporated. All of these properties relate to discussions in the previous unit, "Energy and the Atmosphere," where we've seen that the presence of nearby bodies of water tends to smooth out large swings of temperature.

We also use water as the standard for measuring temperature. Water **changes phases** from a liquid to a solid (or vice versa) at 0°C and changes between liquid and gaseous phases at 100°C. Here again, water breaks the rules. Most substances steadily get denser and heavier as their temperature decreases. *Water is most dense, and thus heaviest, at 4°C.* The liter is defined as the volume occupied by 1,000 grams of water at 4°C. Water expands and gets lighter both above and below this temperature. This property allows water in its solid phase, ice, to float on liquid water. When bodies of water like lakes get cold, they freeze at the top first, and rarely, if at all, freeze solid—a very fortunate circumstance for aquatic creatures. Water can exist for quite some time over a fairly broad range of temperatures in all three phases simultaneously. (Think about visiting the North Pole supported by a ship on liquid water, watching glaciers float by, as you breathe a nice whiff of moist ocean air.)

Earth's Water Reservoirs

Where can we find Earth's water? Looking at a map or globe of the earth, it's easy to see that much of the surface of our planet is covered with water—more than 71%, in fact. The salt water of Earth's oceans accounts for 97% of all the water in the **hydrosphere** (see page 23). Geologists also believe there is more than that amount of water chemically combined with the rocks in earth's **mantle**, but most of that water is forever unavailable.

Three percent of earth's water is **fresh water**. Two-thirds of this fresh water is currently frozen as **ice** at the earth's poles and on its mountaintops. That means that all of the **rivers**, **lakes**, **water vapor**, and **groundwater** spread around the planet represents less than 1% of Earth's total water supply. This is the fraction of earth's water that land-based creatures can use—their **fresh water reservoir**.

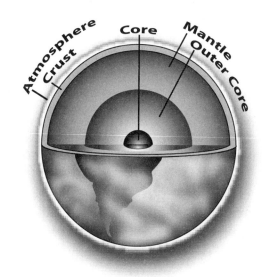

The earth's atmosphere holds an amazing amount of fresh water. Every 13 hours, a body of water the size of Lake Erie, one of the Great Lakes, rises into the sky. When water falls as rain on dry land, it collects in rivers and lakes as **runoff**. The five Great Lakes of North America hold 18% of all the world's surface fresh water, some 25 trillion tons. Still, all of Earth's runoff amounts to one-third of one percent of all fresh water. Lakes and streams meet most of our immediate water demands, including 50% of drinking water.

Water that doesn't run off sinks farther into the Earth's crust and collects in porous rock. These reservoirs, called **aquifers**, contain 30 times more water than all of the worlds' lakes and streams combined. Aquifers provide the other half of our drinking water (although in rural areas, they provide 96% in the form of wells). Sixty-five percent of the water used to grow crops comes from underground aquifers. This **groundwater** moves much more slowly than surface water, and, once polluted, is harder to clean up. Much of the groundwater in aquifers in the west comes from glaciers that melted at the end of the last ice age.

Salt Water Tales

Anyone who has accidentally swallowed ocean water knows that it is salty, or **saline**. Every liter (1,000 g) of ocean water contains 35 grams of various "salts" that exist primarily as **ions** (see page 23). Fifty-five percent of these are chloride ions, but other important elements and compounds include potassium (1.1%), calcium (1.2%), sulfate (7.9%), magnesium (3.7%), and NaCl, or table salt (30.6%). Nearly all of these minerals are washed into the world's oceans from the powerful erosive forces of runoff from rivers.

Sea creatures have made good use of dissolved minerals, like silicon and calcium, to make shells and, potassium and calcium, to make bones.

Salt concentrations in the deep ocean basins remain quite constant over long periods of time. Creatures that live in these **marine habitats** have adjusted their physiologies to match. They are not **tolerant** of changes in salt concentration and will die in water without the typical **salinity** (salt content) of 3.5%. The salinity of water varies much more in bays or estuaries that receive lots of fresh water from rivers or in landlocked salty seas where evaporation during warm seasons or extended drought can increase relative salt content. Creatures that have evolved in the latter habitats are more tolerant of shifting salt levels.

Salt affects some of the **physical properties** of water, especially **density**. Anyone who has visited a body of water like the Great Salt Lake in Utah knows that it is much easier to float in water with a high salt content. The dissolved ions give water a **greater weight per volume**, which is the measure of density. If you mix a few tablespoons of salt in a beaker of water with a little food coloring added, and then slowly pour this water into a larger beaker partly filled with fresh water, you will see that the salt water sinks to the bottom.

Water density also changes with **temperature**. Cold water molecules bumble around closer to each other because they have less energy. More water molecules in a given volume mean that water is relatively dense. Heated water molecules zip around faster, knocking their neighbors farther away. Warm water is less dense. We will see shortly how these density shifts impact moving water.

Salt water can be converted back to fresh water by heating it so much that water molecules undergo a **phase change** and **evaporate** (see page 24). If the resulting water-filled air is then cooled, the water will condense to a liquid that is free of salts.

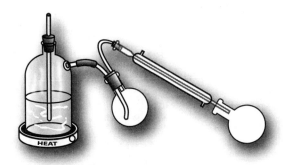

Apparatus for creating fresh water from salt water

Tides and Currents

Water moves. Wind over open water pushes against surface molecules of water that move forward and pile up on neighboring water molecules. This forward motion, combined with friction against the water molecules beneath and gravity, results in water molecules tumbling in loops to create **waves**. As water levels get shallower near shore, increased friction against the sea bottom interrupts the rolling motion, and the waves "break." Surf's up!

Gravitational attractions between the moon and Earth and the Earth-Moon system and the sun cause other familiar and periodic motions of water called **tides**. The moon's mass tugs at both water and land, but water moves more easily. The Earth's oceans "bulge" toward the moon. Maximum attraction occurs when the moon is directly overhead, but maximum tides are delayed four to six hours because of the **inertia of the water**, **friction**, **placement of landmasses**, and the **distance the water must travel**. The sun has a similar effect on water, but, even though it is huge, it's 93 million miles away, so its effect is not very noticeable until the sun, moon, and Earth are aligned. When the moon and the sun "gang up" to tug on Earth's oceans each spring, higher **spring tides** result. When the moon and sun are pulling at right angles to each other, low **neap tides** result.

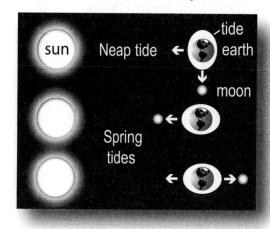

The change in water depth because of high and low tides results in special habitats called **intertidal zones**. The organisms that live here, including creatures like limpets, clams, mussels, barnacles, various crustaceans, starfish, and algae must be especially hardy to deal with life both above and below the sea. Many animals also time their breeding cycles, migrations, and egg-laying behavior to coincide with the cycles of the moon and the tides that result.

We've seen that water density changes with both temperature and salinity. This causes motion beneath the waves called **currents**, which are essentially rivers of moving water within the earth's oceans. See page 19 for the major ocean currents. Wind causes many **surface currents**. These can be important because most of the oceans' tiny producers called **plankton** live in the top 140 meters—the "sunlight zone." All larger ocean creatures depend on this layer, just as terrestrial grazers depend on grass. This interface between water and air is not only a giant "buffet," but it is a nursery for many sea creatures.

Cold water usually sinks, and warm water rises, to create deep current loops that flow in tune with uneven solar heating and the spinning of the earth. When warm surface waters are blown away by winds, cold waters may rise in **upwellings** that often bring nutrients from deep below to feed surface creatures.

The Water Cycle: Travels With Dripp

 Meet Dripp. Dripp is a molecule of water floating in the Gulf of Mexico minding his own business. Like all water, Dripp travels a lot in a process called the **hydrologic cycle**, or **water cycle**, but he always ends up back in the ocean. Let's see how:

As Dripp cruises near the surface of the water, the sun's rays beat down on him. He gets so excited that he crashes into water molecule neighbors willy-nilly, until he **evaporates** into the atmosphere. Ah, room to spare! Dripp rises high into the sky until he begins to feel a bit sluggish and **condenses** onto a particle of dust. Other molecules join him, and he soon finds himself as part of a cloud, drifting inland over Texas.

At first, he's in a high-pressure area, but he soon gets swept up in a current of air that races toward a low-pressure zone in New Mexico. Dripp was looking forward to spending some time as a snowflake in Vail, but instead, close to Santa Fe, New Mexico, a cold air mass tunnels beneath his cloud and shoves him skyward. Bunches of other water molecules climb aboard his dust mote, and pretty soon he's feeling pretty heavy—heavy enough to drop. He does, with a little assistance from **gravity**. He and his dust-mote mates **precipitate** as a drop of rain.

Dripp drops onto a duck's back. You can imagine how slippery that is! Before you know it, he's floating down the Rio Grande. He's nothing but everyday, common **runoff**. "Hey," he thinks, "Don't I even get to see the Grand Canyon? How about a century or ten in a nice quiet **aquifer** or mountain **glacier**?" No such luck! Within a matter of days, he's back with old friends in the Gulf of Mexico. "Quick cycle," they say. "Better luck next time!"

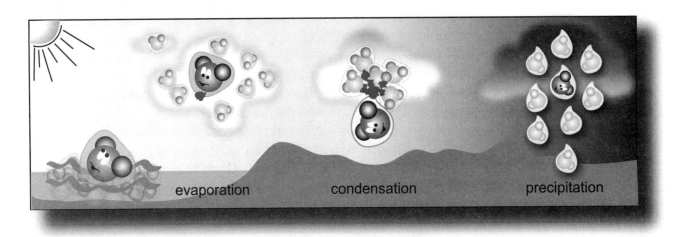

evaporation   condensation   precipitation

On your own paper, write another version of Dripp's journey (starting in the Gulf of Mexico) where he spends some time with the following: Isadore Schlepp, a science teacher, a buffalo named Fred, and a wet gym sock, but eventually ends up in the Gulf of California.

Pollution of Water Resources

 Imagine a day without water, if you can. We use it for drinking, washing, sanitation, and recreation. Farmers need huge quantities of water for growing crops. Business and industry use water in the process of making and selling what we consume. All of this use can result in the **pollution** of water resources unless we use water responsibly.

Water can be polluted by many things. In the past, when water supplies seemed inexhaustible, people just tossed everything into a nearby river and waved goodbye. As recently as 1970, the Cuyahoga River in Ohio was so polluted by industrial and other types of wastes that it literally caught on fire! But the Cuyahoga was saved by laws that regulated the dumping of waste. Water resources can recover if they are treated correctly. Today, everyone lives downstream from someone else.

Rapid increase in **human population** puts a huge stress on water resources. World population has gone from less than 0.5 billion in 1650 to about 3 billion in 1960 to over 6 billion today. Many towns are finding it difficult to treat **human wastewater** before it enters the nearest river. Untreated water leads to the growth of disease-causing microbes that can cause epidemics.

The **agricultural use** of water can cause pollution in two ways:

1. **Pesticides** used to control various insects and other pests get washed into lakes and rivers during runoff. Some of these compounds decompose quickly, while others don't. Some build up in animals and plant tissues and enter our food chain.

2. **Fertilizers** used to increase crop yields contain nitrates that, when flushed into rivers, cause "blooms," or microorganisms in bodies of water that use up oxygen for some creatures and alter habitats in other ways.

Industrial use of water can also add poisons of various kinds to water supplies, as well as petroleum by-products that may coat the surface or physically impair wildlife. Certain medical wastes can add potentially dangerous pathogens to water supplies. In addition, just the excess **heat** added to rivers and other bodies of water can adversely affect the animals and plants that live in such water habitats.

Dumps of all sorts including radioactive wastes, mine tailings, and urban landfills, unless monitored carefully, can contribute toxins to groundwater over the years as rainwater leaches these materials into the soils beneath them. It's up to each of us to dispose of household chemicals, pesticides, fertilizers, and assorted "junk" in ways that won't impact the water supplies of our human relatives downstream. Likewise, we hope that our neighbors upstream are doing the same for us.

Human Impact on Water Reserves

Human use of water, especially for irrigation and generation of power, has allowed for the rapid growth and prosperity of human populations. This good news must be tempered with impacts on the environment, both short- and long-term.

Surface water: Most of the 3.2 million miles of waterways in the United States have been dammed, drained, or diverted in some way. The Yellowstone River is the only river in the Continental United States over 600 miles long that has not been altered. We use more water for generating electricity than for any other purpose.

The use of **hydroelectric power** in the Columbia River basin in the northwestern United States brought much-needed power to the region, but damming the river has disrupted fish migrations, including that of the commercially important salmon. Many dams, reservoirs, and at least thirty power plants dot the course of the Colorado River, the main source of surface water for the American southwest. This river that carved the Grand Canyon gets used so heavily that it barely trickles into the sea. The Lake Powell reservoir behind the Glen Canyon dam resulted in the loss of a large stretch of canyon lands. Dams also prevent normal flooding cycles that affect downstream river habitats, so dams may be opened periodically to create man-made floods.

Draining swamps, bogs, and coastal marshes in the nineteenth and early twentieth centuries claimed land for agriculture and settlement, but we now know that **wetlands** are important not only as wildlife sanctuaries, but as a natural means of cleaning water of pollutants.

Groundwater: Groundwater supplies in California and the Midwest have made American farms the most productive in the world, but withdrawals from this "water bank" exceed deposits. This will break the "water bank" in the future unless corrected. The northern Midwest aquifer near Chicago dropped 1,000 feet at one point, but when domestic use switched to Lake Michigan, water levels rebounded at least 250 feet. In California, however, groundwater used for farming has caused the land in the San Joaquin Valley to drop thirty feet since the 1920s because the subterranean layers of clay holding the water collapsed. This water can't be totally replenished. Water levels have also dropped sharply in the high plains Ogallala aquifer, important in western grain-growing states.

Some good news: Industrial growth has quadrupled in size since 1950, but water use has decreased 19% because people have learned to use water more efficiently. New laws require domestic plumbing to do a better job. "Low flow" toilets, for example, use only 1.6 gallons per flush instead of 3.5–7 gallons. We all need to become better stewards for Dripp and his friends!

Name: _____ Date: _____

Part 3: Sailing in the Hydrosphere
Putting It All Together

CONTENT REVIEW

1. Water is a _____ compound made up of _____

    and _____. Because it has a positive and negative end, it is a

    _____ molecule.

2. T or F? Compared to other compounds, water is quick to heat up and quick to cool down.

3. Groundwater collects in porous rock reservoirs called _____.

4. T or F? Approximately 3% of the water on Earth is fresh water.

5. Water is unusual because:

    A. It is not a very good solvent.

    B. It is less dense as a solid than a liquid.

    C. It evaporates at such a low temperature.

    D. It is a non-polar ionic compound.

6. When the earth, moon, and sun are aligned, you can expect a high _____

    tide.

7. When liquid water heats up, it eventually _____. When water vapor cools,

    it _____ and will fall as _____.

8. Water may get polluted with _____ or _____ when they are

    used to grow crops.

9. Name two kinds of surface water. _____   _____

10. The salinity of water affects the _____ of water, making it easier to float in

    salt water.

11. Neap tides (extra low) result when the _____ and _____ are

    pulling at right angles to each other.

12. Water molecules are "sticky" because the negative oxygen end of one molecule tends

    to form weak _____ _____ with the two positive hydrogen

    atoms of another molecule.

Name: _____ Date: _____

Part 3: Sailing in the Hydrosphere: Putting It All Together (cont.)

CONCEPT REVIEW

1. Why would it be more difficult to clean a polluted aquifer than a polluted river?

   _____

   _____

2. Silica gel, a drying agent, is often provided with cameras and other expensive equipment that might rust. How do you suppose it's similar to the salt that is spread on dirt roads?

   _____

   _____

3. Explain why lakes freeze from the top down. _____

   _____

4. Why is water called the universal solvent? _____

   _____

   _____

5. Sharks live in marine habitats. Would you expect them to be more or less tolerant to changes in salinity than a clam that lives in an estuary? _____

   Why? _____

   _____

6. If the earth had no large moon, explain what tides would be like. _____

   _____

   _____

7. Why is it difficult to know just how long a particular water molecule will take to complete "one loop" in the water cycle? _____

   _____

8. Why might trash dumps cause less pollution over a period of ten years in a desert than in a Midwestern forest? _____

   _____

9. T or F? Groundwater reservoirs can, in part, be replenished.

Part 4: Earth's Cosmic Neighborhood
The Parts of a Solar System

The sun's glare overpowers any other source of light in the daytime sky. It's not until our side of the earth turns its back to the sun that we see that other objects reside there as well—the flickering light of **stars**, the huge disk of the **moon**, and the smaller, steadily shining disks of nearby **planets**. The stars are other distant suns, glowing from the heat produced by nuclear reactions at their centers. The immense gravity generated by our nearby star, the sun, holds the earth, its moon, an assortment of planets, and a host of less massive objects in a tight grip. The sun, plus this collection of objects, is called the **solar system**.

Although planets look much like stars in the night sky, they differ in several ways:

1. Planets move against the backdrop of stars, evidence that they are much closer than stars.
2. Planets (and their moons) shine from sunlight reflected off their surface, not self-generated energy.
3. This nearby reflected light is brighter than distant starlight, so planets don't appear to flicker as stars do in the night sky.

Many planets have **moons**, which are small bodies under their gravitational influence. Most moons are small compared to their planet. Our moon, one-fourth the size of Earth, is an exception.

We can break our solar system into three zones based roughly on temperature:

Zone 1, closest to the sun, is too warm for much water to exist as solid ice. Four planets formed here that are mostly made of rocky silicate minerals. **Mercury**, closest to the sun, shows a cratered surface with no atmosphere. **Venus**, orbiting between Mercury and Earth, has a dense atmosphere of carbon dioxide with clouds of sulfuric acid. Then, beyond **Earth** is the red planet, **Mars**, with a thin atmosphere and a little ice and frozen carbon dioxide at its poles. A ring of rocky rubble called the **asteroid belt** circles at the edge of Zone 1.

Zone 2 contains several large **gas giant planets**, largely composed of hydrogen and helium. **Jupiter**, the most massive, may have kept the material in the asteroid belt from forming another planet. **Saturn**, next in line, has at least 31 moons and a set of distinctive rings formed of ice and dust particles. **Uranus** has a smaller ring system, not discovered until the twentieth century. **Neptune** follows, similar to **Uranus** in size and composition, but much colder. Small and icy **Pluto** orbits beyond Neptune (most of its year). Some astronomers argue that it's not big enough to be called a planet.

At least 200 million icy, asteroid-sized objects orbit the sun in **Zone 3** beyond Pluto in the **Kuiper belt**—the source of short-period ice and dust balls called **comets**, whose orbits take 200 years or less. The sun also holds billions, possibly trillions, of icy bodies in the **Oort cloud**, the source of long-period comets. The sun evaporates incoming comet material to form brushy "tails."

Our System's Place in the Cosmos

Our sun and its system of planets is not unique. Although most **extrasolar planets** (those outside our solar system) that have been discovered so far are Jupiter-sized or larger (because current methods depend on the "wobble" such planets cause in their stars' motion), there's no reason to think that smaller rocky bodies don't exist as well. Stars condense from clouds of dust and gas. Planets, asteroids, and comets are leftover clumps and fragments of the sun-making process.

The few thousand stars you can see with the naked eye can be pretty impressive, especially when no city lights or clouds obstruct your view. Stars shine in such numbers in one strip across the sky that they look like spilled milk: the **Milky Way**. Many more stars pop into view through a telescope, yet, until 1924, astronomers thought all the stars belonged to one huge congregation called the **Milky Way galaxy**. In 1924, astronomer Edwin Hubble showed that some "clouds" or nebulae were actually other, distant galaxies not unlike our Milky Way. He was able to do this using the light emission characteristics of certain **cepheid variable stars** as distance yardsticks. Now, through the space telescope named after Hubble, in any given small segment of the sky, it is possible to see thousands of galaxies scattered like diamond dust on black velvet.

But let's concentrate for a moment on our own Milky Way galaxy. This collection of a few hundred *billion* stars orbits around a center in a huge flat disk that probably looks very much like a close neighbor, the **Andromeda galaxy**. The disk is not uniform, but instead consists of thick, **spiral arms** that contain thicker bunches of stars. Our sun resides in the Orion spiral arm, a "comfortable" distance from the galactic center. The galactic center appears to be a zone of fantastic energies, dense stars, and matter collapsed into an object so massive that light can no longer escape from it. Such an object is referred to as a **black hole.** The picture at the right shows where our solar system is located within the Milky Way galaxy.

Milky Way Galaxy

The picture below shows the zones of our solar system.

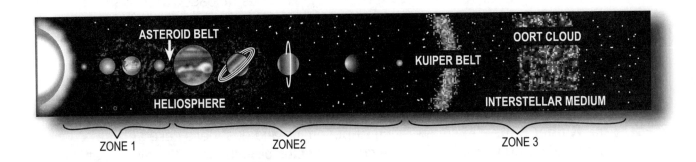

Name: _____ Date: _____

Sizes and Distances in Our Solar System

At 750 miles per hour, a plane can fly from coast to coast in about four hours. Not bad! It would take that same plane fourteen years to fly the 93,000,000 miles (149,600,000 km) from Earth to the sun (certainly running out of peanuts and soda pop in the process). Besides, it's difficult to deal with millions of anything! For distances within and beyond our solar system, two other units of measure are useful: the **astronomical unit** (**AU**) and the **light-year**.

One AU is the distance from Earth to the sun. Thus, our planetary neighbor Mars is 1.52 AU from the sun, while distant Pluto is 39.4 AU from the sun. (You could fly there in just 552 years on your favorite air carrier.) The distance of the various planets from the sun (and other statistics) are given in the "Planetary Fast Facts" table below.

A light-year is the distance light travels in one year, zipping along at 186,000 miles (300,000 kilometers) per second.

PLANETARY FAST FACTS						
Planet	**Year**	**# of Moons**	**Diameter (km)**	**Rotation**	**Mass**	**# of AU's from sun**
Mercury	88 days	0	4,880	59 days	0.55E	0.39
Venus	226 days	0	12,104	243 days	0.8E	0.72
Earth	365.2 days	1	12,756	23.9 hours	1*	1.0
Mars	687 days	2	6,794	24.6 hours	0.1E	1.52
Jupiter	11.9 years	63	142,984	9.9 hours	318E	5.20
Saturn	29.5 years	31	120,536	10.7 hours	95E	9.54
Uranus	84 years	27	51,118	17.3 hours	14.5E	19.18
Neptune	165 years	13	49,532	16.1 hours	17.1E	30.06
Pluto	148 years	1	2,484	6.4 days	0.002E	39.44

* Masses are given in fractions or multiples of Earth's mass, which is 6×10^{21} metric tons.
 <u>Sun statistics</u>: The sun rotates in 25 days (at the equator); its diameter is 1,390,000 km; and its mass is 333,000 times that of Earth. It has a temperature of 15 million°C at the core, but only 5,500°C at the surface.

To get a picture in your mind of the relative distances of the planets from the sun, let's think football fields, which are a hundred yards long. One AU is going to equal 2.54 yards (100 divided by 39.44 AU, the distance to Pluto). Assume that the sun burns at one goal line. Mercury will orbit less than half a yard from the sun; Venus will be about three-fourths of a yard away. Earth, of course, is on the two-and-a-half yard line. Jupiter lies just over the 13-yard mark (2.54 yards/AU x 5.2 AU).

APPLY:

1. Using the table above, calculate how many yards down the field each of these planets will be found. Saturn _____ Uranus _____ Neptune _____

2. Jupiter's diameter is 142,984 km (see the table above). Let that diameter equal 90 mm and, on your own paper, draw all nine planets in the solar system to the same scale. (Hint: Divide 142,984 by 90 to find out how many kilometers are represented by each millimeter.)

Planets, Moons, and Rings

Every planet in our solar system condensed out of the same cloud of dust and gas as our sun. How did the 138 known natural **satellites** called **moons** orbiting those various planets form? Some of the largest ones, those circling gas giant planets like **Jupiter** and **Saturn**, may be "leftovers" from the parent planet's formation. Other moons—perhaps even our own—resulted from titanic **collisions** during the rough-and-tumble beginnings of the solar system. A large planet may also **capture** small bodies that pass too close to them with the force of their gravitational attraction. These bodies may become permanent satellites or get torn apart by gravitational stresses and become **rings**.

Jupiter and Saturn, composed mostly of hydrogen and helium, and the first- and second-biggest planets in our neighborhood, between them have 94 of our solar system's moons. **Galileo Galilei** (1564–1642) discovered Jupiter's four biggest moons in 1610 with a telescope of his own design. **Io**, Jupiter's innermost moon, possesses nearly the same mass as Earth's moon. Jupiter's enormous gravity tugs on Io with such force that Io's innards churn with hot molten energy. Loki, one of Io's hundred known active volcanoes, emits more heat than all of Earth's volcanoes combined.

The surface of **Europa**, the next-closest moon to Jupiter, excites scientists because its shiny, crumpled features resemble ice flows on Earth. Movement beneath the surface pushes these flows around and may represent currents in a huge subsurface ocean, warmed by some of the same stresses Io endures. Where there is water, scientists think there might be life.

A magnetic field arches around our solar system's largest moon, **Ganymede**, the only moon known to have a **magnetosphere** like Earth. Ganymede is larger than either Mercury or Pluto. Ganymede's low density implies the presence of water, and active tectonic plates may have crumpled its rough surface.

Saturn may be number two in the size department, but it does have some impressive rings composed of dust, rocks, and frozen ice that stretch to a diameter of 282,000 km. Some of its moons—or perhaps passing asteroids or comets—apparently strayed too close and gravitation stresses pulled them apart into particles that orbit in a layer from 10 meters to one kilometer thick. Small moons called **shepherd moons** clear out gaps in the rings through their gravitational influence. The Italian astronomer **Giovanni Cassini** discovered the biggest ring gap in 1675, which is now called the **Cassini division**.

The *Cassini* **spacecraft** left Earth in 1997 and arrived at Saturn on June 30, 2004. The craft released the **Huygens** probe, which successfully landed on the surface of **Titan**, our solar system's second-largest moon. Titan is rich in hydrocarbons with a thick nitrogen atmosphere.

APPLY:

1. The moon Ganymede has a _____ or magnetic field around it.

2. Of what are the rings of Saturn composed? _____

_____

The Earth-Moon "Double Planet" System

Many years ago, Earth may have been involved in a celestial "train wreck" with another body about the size of the planet Mars. That collision sprayed rock and hot vapors into space that later pulled together in a clump that would become Earth's moon—a body one-fourth of Earth's diameter and one-eightieth of its mass. This theory seems to best explain the moon's composition, orbit, and relatively large size compared to Earth. Our moon is the fifth-largest in our solar system.

The moon would have loomed large in the sky of ancient Earth. The gravitational tug-of-war between Earth and the moon causes the moon to slowly spiral away from Earth. The moon recedes from Earth today at a rate of 3.8 cm per year and orbits at an average distance of 384,400 km. No need to worry, though. The sun will burn out before the earth and moon can break up their relationship.

Earth's stronger gravitational pull has also coupled the moon's **rotation** (spin) and its revolution about the earth, so Earth observers like us always see the same side of the moon. The Russian spacecraft *Luna 3* first photographed the moon's crater-pocked backside in 1959. The moon's gravitational pull puts a brake on Earth's rotation.

The moon also tends to keep the earth from "wobbling" very much as it spins on its axis. Mars, for example, only has two tiny moons and tends to wobble much more. This makes Mars' seasonal shifts in temperature more severe. Having milder seasons on Earth may have helped life thrive here.

The moon's overall composition resembles that of Earth's **mantle**, one of the observations that supports an impact theory for its origin. However, moon rocks are richer in aluminum, calcium, and titanium than the earth and poorer in silver, zinc, and gold. The moon's average density is also similar to that of Earth's outer layers. When moon rock cooled in the distant past, it solidified into unique rock called **KREEP**. *K* stands for the element *potassium*, *REE* stands for *Rare Earth Elements*, and *P* stands for the element *phosphorus*.

Although the moon never had liquid water, the spacecraft *Clementine* surprised scientists in 1994 when it discovered ice at the moon's poles. Sunlight couldn't evaporate this water, which was tucked away in the depths of shadowy craters. Temperatures in the shade on the moon dip to -169°C but zoom up to 117°C in full sunlight—another effect of having no atmosphere around which to spread the heat. This water, not to mention the craters that keep it refrigerated, may have come from comets, which brings us to the subject of impacts and collisions. Our solar system still provides some surprises from time to time.

APPLY:

1. How far will the moon have receded from the earth in 1,000 years?

   _____

2. How much do temperatures vary between the sunlight and shade on the moon?

   _____

Impacts and Collisions, Past and Present

Asteroids, meteors, and other debris pelted the earth and moon during their early, "formative" years, gouging out many **craters**, large and small. Without an atmosphere and no life to smooth out its scars, the moon looks like an overused target on a rifle range. Only very large and/or recent craters on Earth—like Meteor Crater in Arizona—are visible. Wind, rain, and water have smoothed Earth's ancient wounds. Impacts also created the moon's mountains, instead of the collision of tectonic plates, as on Earth. While the moon's deep interior is still molten, its surface is cold and rigid, only suffering fairly mild "moonquakes" now and then, largely caused by Earth's pull.

The moon's past volcanic activity, however, formed what are now referred to as lunar "seas," because that's what they looked like to early astronomers. *Mare Imbrium*, Latin for *Sea of Rains*, forms the right eye of the "man in the moon." An asteroid apparently collided with the moon in the past. Volcanic lava oozed into the resulting crater, smoothing its floor when it hardened. The left eye formed from a similar impact, creating *Mare Serenitatis*, which is Latin for *Sea of Serenity*. The crust on the moon's backside is thicker, and less volcanic activity occurred there to smooth out its "wrinkles."

Although impacts and collisions on both the earth and moon were much more frequent in the past, they still continue. Recall that lots of rocks and "dirty snowballs" orbit the distant **Kuiper belt** and **Oort cloud** (see page 33). Many of these objects have very elongated orbits that bring them close to the sun on long-term schedules. The **asteroid belt** between Mars and Jupiter also contains millions of objects from 100 meters to 1,000 meters in size, The planets move like gravitational elephants among these objects, every now and then bumping smaller bodies into different orbits. Massive objects from outside the solar system may also pass close enough to the Kuiper belt and Oort cloud to nudge a few objects sunward. This results in occasional impacts and collisions.

In 1994, scientists got a rare chance to observe the collision of a comet with the planet Jupiter. **Comet Shoemaker-Levy 9** strayed too close to Jupiter and broke into many fragments, some as large as 1.5 kilometers across. These "fragments" struck with the force of 100 billion tons or more of TNT.

At one time, a six-mile-long object struck the earth near what is now the Yucatán Peninsula of Mexico, creating the 170-kilometer-wide Cicxulub Crater. This not only caused immediate death and destruction, but it changed the climate long enough to help cause the extinction of 60% of the species alive at the time, including the dinosaurs. Later, a much smaller object struck the earth, forming Meteor Crater in Arizona. Heads up, everyone!

Rotations and Revolutions: Days and Seasons

A planet **rotates** on its **axis**, an invisible line drawn between its north and south poles, which results in days and nights for an observer on the planet's surface. However, a planet **revolves** around the sun in a yearly cycle that produces **seasons**. Let's check this out with some fruit, a pushpin or thumbtack, and a light bulb.

APPLY:

Rotation—making night and day: Take an apple from the fruit bowl to represent Earth. The stem end and the opposite "old-flower" end will be the poles. Stick a pushpin or thumbtack (That will be you, the earthly observer!) into the apple somewhere between the poles. Put a lamp without a lampshade in the middle of the room to represent the sun. Turn off the rest of the lights in the room.

Let the side of the apple with the pushpin face the "sun." Imagine that you are a flea sitting on that pushpin. Looking up, you admire the sun directly overhead at noon. Notice that half the apple, the "daylight side," shines with reflected light. The other, the "night side" is in shadow. The shadow ends at a line called the **terminator**. Slowly rotate the apple. Notice how the pushpin flea approaches the terminator. What does the sun appear to do from the flea's point of view? When you reach the terminator, enjoy the brief sunset. Continue to rotate the apple, carrying the flea through Apple-Earth night. When will sunrise occur?

Revolution—making the seasons: The stem end of Apple-Earth will be the North Pole. Tilt it a little toward the sun. The earth's axis is tilted at an angle of 23.5°, "wobbling" over a period of years from 21.75° to 24.5°. Notice that the North Pole is in daylight all of the time as you rotate Apple-Earth to make day and night. This is what happens on Earth during summer in the Northern Hemisphere.

Keeping Apple-Earth tilted the same way, begin moving in a circle around the sun to start an Apple-Earth yearly revolution. When you have moved one-fourth of the way around the circle (90°), stop and look at the terminator. It passes through both poles. You have arrived at the first day of Apple-Earth autumn. Move another quarter of the way around the sun (directly across the room from where you started). Note that now the South Pole of Apple-Earth is pointing toward the sun. That hemisphere will get more daily sunlight, creating summer there, but winter in the Northern Hemisphere. The apple's stem is in shadow all day. Continue moving in a circle around the sun. When will spring arrive? (see page 20)

The earth takes 365.2 days to make this journey. It also travels in a "slightly squashed circle" called an **ellipse** (see page 42) that puts the Northern Hemisphere farthest from the sun during its summer. The axis swivels over thousands of years. Long-term axis swivels and wobbles and slight orbit changes help explain why "ice ages" tend to occur over a long period of time.

The Phases of the Moon

 The moon, like the earth, other planets and their moons, asteroids, and comets, can only shine by reflected sunlight. Because our moon is so close, we see it move through different phases as it revolves around the earth every 29.5 days and changes its position relative to the sun.

APPLY:

To demonstrate this, let's trade in the Apple-Earth used on the previous page for a Soccer Ball-Earth. Find a tennis ball to represent the moon. Keep the same light source for the sun. Also find a friend to hold either the earth or the moon. Use a marker to put a happy face on a tennis ball. This will represent the "man in the moon" image marked by *Mare Imbrium* and *Mare Serenitatis* (see page 38). Remember, the moon always keeps its same side facing Earth.

Let "moon person" stand so he or she can place the tennis ball between Soccer Ball-Earth and the sun. (The sun, moon, and Earth don't necessarily have to be in a direct line.) What will an observer on Earth see when looking up toward the moon? Nothing—at least, not much. Sometimes, you can faintly see the moon by light reflected off the earth called **earthshine**. This moon is called a **new moon**.

Move the moon slowly around the Earth less than one-quarter revolution. Note how, from the perspective of Soccer Ball-Earth, you will see more and more light reflected in ever-expanding slivers. During the first seven days after a new moon, the moon becomes a **waxing crescent**. (*Waxing* means enlarging or expanding.) After a one-quarter revolution, you can see half the moon's face from Soccer Ball-Earth. This is the **first quarter moon**.

Move the moon a little farther along its path around Earth. More and more of its face becomes visible as the **waxing gibbous moon**. Finally, when the moon reaches the spot where Earth lies between it and the sun, all of its face is illuminated as a **full moon**. As the moon continues to move, the area visible becomes less and less, creating the **waning gibbous moon**. (*Waning* means shrinking.) The **last quarter moon** appears when the moon has completed three-fourths of a revolution. Over the last week of the lunar month, the quarter moon shrinks to form a **waning crescent moon** before the next new moon.

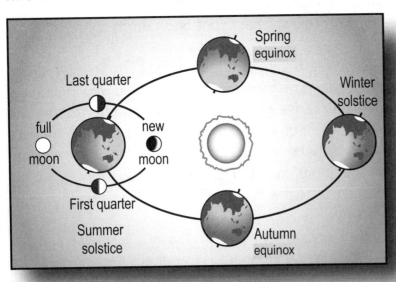

Eclipses—Solar and Lunar

APPLY: Keep your soccer ball, tennis ball, and light source handy from the previous page as we discuss **eclipses**—events where one heavenly body passes through the shadow of another.

Turn on your "sun" in a dark room. Stand near a wall and hold Soccer Ball-Earth to one side. It casts a clear, dark shadow on the wall. The earth casts a dark shadow in space that astronomers call an **umbra**, the Latin word for *shadow*. Because the real earth has an atmosphere that scatters light, it also casts a fuzzy shadow outside the umbra called the **penumbra**. Since the moon orbits the earth, its motion will sometimes carry it into one or both shadows, creating a **total lunar eclipse**, if it falls completely into the umbra and a **partial lunar eclipse** if it doesn't.

1. Under what conditions will the moon miss the earth's shadow?_____

_____

_____

_____

_____

ABSORB: Note that a lunar eclipse will always occur on or very near a full moon (see above). Have someone hold Soccer Ball-Earth and move Tennis Ball-Moon so you can see why this is so. During a total lunar eclipse, the moon glows a deep coppery red from scattered Earth light. Lunar eclipses can be seen from any point on Earth where the moon is visible, and they tend to occur about once or twice a year on average.

During solar eclipses, the earth passes into a shadow cast by the moon. Move Tennis Ball-Moon to a position between your sunlight source and Soccer Ball-Earth to see how this works. **Solar eclipses** occur around or during new moons. By chance, the apparent size of the sun and the moon are nearly identical when the sun and moon are relatively close to the earth during winter in the Northern Hemisphere. When the moon totally blocks out the brightest part of the sun or **photosphere** during a **total solar eclipse**, all you can see is the glowing outer solar layer called the **corona**. The corona glows with large brilliant spikes when sunspot activity is high and is not much more than a faint band of light when sunspots are absent.

The moon casts a shadow on the earth 270 km wide, traveling at a speed of 1,700 km/h. Thus, an observer must lie directly in the path of this shadow to see a total eclipse from the ground. You will see a **partial solar eclipse** when only a portion of the shadow passes over. When the moon is farthest from the earth in its orbit, its apparent size as it passes between Earth and sun is just slightly smaller than the sun, resulting in a bright ring of light during totality called an **annular eclipse**.

Do not look directly at a solar eclipse. Permanent eye damage may result. Only look at solar eclipses through special sunglasses or by casting its light through a pinhole onto paper.

Gravity and the Movements of the Planets

The sun, stars, and planets rise and set every day. It's easy for humans to believe that these celestial objects are all small things orbiting around us and our world, the earth. And that's what people did think for most of human history. **Nicolaus Copernicus** (1473–1543) dared to think "outside the box" (and the teachings of the Catholic Church at the time) and proposed that the sun, not the earth, was the object around which all heavenly bodies in our solar system turned. His idea was not a guess. It explained age-old observations about the planetary motions in a simple and direct way. A mathematician among the next generation of scientists, **Johannes Kepler** (1571–1630), was able to describe planetary motions precisely with his three laws.

Kepler's three laws are:

1. **The orbit of a planet about the sun is an ellipse** (an oval) **with the sun at one focus.** To make an ellipse, stick two pins in a piece of cardboard. These are the two foci. Tie the ends of a piece of string together to make a loop wider than the distance between the pins. Put the loop over the pins and pull it tight with the writing end of a pencil in contact with the cardboard. Keeping tension on the loop, move the pencil around the pins, and you will draw an ellipse.

2. **A line joining a planet and the sun sweeps out equal areas in equal intervals of time.** This means that a planet will move more quickly when it is closer to the sun and more slowly when it is farther away.

3. **The square of the time it takes a planet to move around the sun is directly proportional to the cube of the average distance of the planet from the sun:** (planet's year)^2 is proportional to (average distance from sun)^3.

The physicist **Sir Isaac Newton** (1642–1727) was able to connect Kepler's laws to his own observations on force and motion and show that all masses, whether they were the size of planets or soccer balls or sand grains, were attracted to each other with a force that was inversely proportional to the square of the distance between them. In other words, two masses have the most attraction to each other at close range, and that attraction rapidly drops off with distance. **($F = GM_1M_2/d^2$) M_1** and **M_2** are two masses, **d** is the distance between them and **G** is a term called the gravitational constant that was determined by experimentation.

Kepler didn't spend all of his time playing with numbers, however. **Galileo** (see page 36) sent him one of his "new-fangled" telescopes to look at the moon, stars, and planets. Kepler wrote *Somnium*, a story about an imaginary trip to the moon, which was most likely the first science fiction story ever written.

Name: _____ Date: _____

Part 4: Earth's Cosmic Neighborhood
Putting It All Together

APPLY:

CONTENT REVIEW

1. Our sun and other _____ produce their own light. _____ and their _____ only shine by light reflected from the sun.

2. T or F? Our solar system is larger than most galaxies.

3. Give the distance from the earth to the sun in astronomical units. _____

4. Planets acquire moons that orbit around them:

   A. After collisions with large objects.

   B. When moons pass too close to a planet's gravitational field.

   C. During the process of condensation from gas when the solar system formed.

   D. All of the above.

5. The Earth-Moon system could be referred to as a "double planet," because

   _____.

6. The Sea of Rains on Earth's moon is actually a large depression filled with

   _____.

7. A planet _____ on its axis, but _____ around the sun.

8. Describe the difference between a new moon and a full moon. _____

   _____

9. T or F? When the moon passes between the earth and the sun, you may see a lunar eclipse.

10. Nicolaus Copernicus proposed that the center of the solar system was the _____ not the earth.

11. The "slightly squashed circle" that is the shape of a planet's orbit is called an

    _____.

12. Of what is the moon rock KREEP composed? _____

    _____

Name: _____ Date: _____

Part 4: Earth's Cosmic Neighborhood
Putting It All Together (cont.)

CONCEPT REVIEW

1. How would the length of a "year" on an asteroid orbiting in the asteroid belt between Mars and Jupiter compare with the length of our year on Earth? _____

_____

_____

2. T or F? It's very likely that most stars have nine planets orbiting them.

3. If our neighbor galaxy, the Andromeda galaxy, is like the Milky Way galaxy, there is a massive _____ _____ at its center.

4. Would it be better to measure the distance to a star halfway across the Milky Way in light-years or astronomical units? _____ Why? _____

_____

_____

5. If a massive object passed close to Jupiter's innermost moon, Io, and bumped it into an orbit closer to Jupiter, what might you expect to happen? _____

_____ Why? _____

_____

6. The planet Zugor's axis is not tilted at all with respect to its star. What would you expect the seasons to be like on Zugor? _____

_____

_____

7. Marvin claimed to have seen the most beautiful lunar eclipse. He described the crescent moon slowly turning a deep emerald green. What two things are wrong with Marvin's description? _____ _____

8. T or F? Two soccer balls would have a greater gravitational attraction to each other when they are 20 meters apart rather than when they are two meters apart.

Answer Keys

The Rock Cycle (p. 8)
1. A. weathering and erosion
   B. compaction and cementation
2. heat and pressure, melt
3. cool and harden
4. metamorphic
5. F
6. minerals
7. gneiss
8. clastic, organic

Part 1: Earth—A Wild and Changing Planet: Putting It All Together (pgs. 11–12)
CONTENT REVIEW
1. (Any order) fault, fold, or fracture
2. F
3. T
5. (Any 4) color, streak, hardness, crystal shape, luster, density, cleavage, magnetism, radioactivity
6. Igneous rocks have completely melted and cooled; sedimentary rocks form from sedimentation and compression; metamorphic rocks can originally be igneous or sedimentary, but are changed by heat and pressure.
7. F
8. chemical
9. Stable
10. Extrusive
CONCEPT REVIEW
1. More slowly because the interior of Mars is colder and the atmosphere is thin (little weathering)
2. Louisiana, because more deposition is occurring there.
3. A
4. (Any 3) Fingernail, iron nail, glass, knife blade, steel file
5. Convergent plate boundary
6. Head for high ground in the case of a tsunami.
7. F   8. T

Predicting the Weather (p. 18)
Symbols are mixed and on the same side of the line because occluded fronts are mixtures of warm and cold air masses moving in the same direction; stationary fronts have warm and cold front symbols on opposite sides of the line because warm and cold air masses are pushing against each, but going nowhere.

Part 2: Energy and the Atmosphere: Putting It All Together (p. 21–22)
CONTENT REVIEW
1. (Any order) convection, conduction, and radiation
2. (Any order) temperature, altitude (or elevation), and moisture content (or humidity)
3. F
4. dew point
5. T
6. B
7. latitude, sea level, water (in that order)
8. F
9. F
10. windward
CONCEPT REVIEW
1. F
2. decrease
3. More ultraviolet radiation would reach Earth, harming some creatures.
4. Few winds for sailing in the doldrums
5. It compares the temperature difference between wet bulb and dry bulb thermometers
6. Rain gear
7. From the southeast
8. It would get much colder.
9. Juanita, because water tends to moderate temperatures.
10. T

Part 3: Sailing in the Hydrosphere: Putting It All Together (p. 31–32)
CONTENT REVIEW
1. covalent, hydrogen, oxygen; polar
2. F
3. aquifers
4. T
5. B
6. spring
7. evaporates, condenses, precipitation
8. (Any order) fertilizers, pesticides
9. (Any 2, rivers and lakes preferred) rivers, lakes, ponds, streams, swamps, bogs
10. density
11. (Any order) moon, sun
12. hydrogen bonds
CONCEPT REVIEW
1. The water in an aquifer is more difficult to reach and doesn't recycle as quickly.
2. It absorbs excess water vapor.

Answer Keys

3. Ice is less dense than liquid water and rises to the top.
4. The charged ends of water molecules tug apart the charged atoms in ionic compounds, so water is capable of dissolving many substances.
5. Less tolerant because they have evolved in a stable saline environment
6. Smaller tides would be caused by a distant sun.
7. It depends on whether the water gets locked in long-term reservoirs.
8. Less movement of pollutants into aquifers and rivers
9. T

Sizes and Distances in the Solar System (p. 35)
1. Saturn: 24.2 yards; Uranus: 48.7 yards; Neptune: 76.4 yards
2. 1 mm = 1,589 km. Mercury: 3 mm, Venus: 7.6 mm, Earth: 8 mm, Mars: 4.3 mm, Jupiter: 90 mm, Saturn: 76 mm, Uranus: 32 mm, Neptune: 31 mm, Pluto: 1.6 mm

Planets, Moons, and Rings (p. 36)
1. magnetosphere
2. dust, rocks, ice

The Earth-Moon "Double Planet" System (p. 37)
1. 3,800 cm or 38 m
2. 286°C

Eclipses—Solar and Lunar (p. 41)
1. The moon will miss Earth's shadow sometimes because its orbit is tilted with respect to Earth's orbit around the sun.

Part 4: Earth's Cosmic Neighborhood: Putting It All Together (p. 43–44)
CONTENT REVIEW
1. stars, planets, moons
2. F
3. 1 AU
4. D
5. The moon is so large relative to Earth's size.
6. lava
7. rotates, revolves
8. A new moon is dark because it lies between the sun and the earth; a full moon displays its entire face because Earth is between it and the sun.
9. F
10. sun
11. ellipse
12. potassium, rare earth elements, and phosphorus
CONCEPT REVIEW
1. An asteroid's year would be longer.
2. F
3. black hole
4. In light-years, astronomical units would be too small.
5. If the moon got too close to Jupiter, it would break up and form a ring. This may be what happened to Saturn.
6. Very little seasonal changes
7. The moon would be full and not a crescent; it would appear coppery in color, not green.
8. F